Memory Lane

NORTH SHIELDS

Memory Lane
NORTH SHIELDS

by John Alexander

breedon **books**
PUBLISHING

First published in Great Britain in 2002 by
The Breedon Books Publishing Company Limited
Breedon House, 3 The Parker Centre,
Derby, DE21 4SZ.

ISBN 1 85983 319 5

Printed and bound by Butler & Tanner, Frome, Somerset, England.
Cover printing by Lawrence-Allen Colour Printers, Weston-super-Mare, Somerset.

Contents

Introduction 7

Around North Shields 8

Everyday Life 48

That's Entertainment 93

Schooldays 129

Sporting Days 159

Acknowledgements

The author thanks the following for their help.: Eva Alexander, Stephen Alexander, Jeffrey Alexander, News Guardian & North East Press Limited, Edmund and Harold Atkinson, Frank Wappat, Sid Kerr, King Edward Primary School (Headteacher, Nina Brown), Jean Lines, Ritchie Rutherford, Angus Laverick, The Priory Theatre, Val Whittingham, Steve Arnott, Robert Lewis & the Laurel and Hardy web site, Percy Park Rugby Football Club, North Eastern Co-op, Ray Porter.

Introduction

ANYONE who has read my earlier books will know that this work is my biggest effort yet. Not only is it in hardback but there are twice as many photographs in it compared to the other books.

The task, therefore, of completing *Memory Lane North Shields* on time, within the limited deadline allotted to me, was tough, but the final results are very rewarding. I have to confess there were times when I thought it wouldn't be possible to finish it on time (indeed, complete it at all) but gladly, with the help of North Shields residents who provided many varied and interesting photographic material, I did.

I have tried to provide as much broad material as possible, which includes – aside from pictures – some old posters and newspaper advertisements. The wealth of 'people' photographs number well over 250 alone.

Compiling this book was also different because, although the title states the book is about North Shields, I have slightly widened the scope to include some pictures of interest of Tynemouth and Cullercoats which fall within the geographical area of North Shields. This works better, rather sticking rigidly to 'just' North Shields town centre material.

Vast changes have altered the look of the town. Mass demolition has paved the way for an exciting new future, such as the Royal Quays development.

The first chapter, *Around North Shields*, is essentially a series of town photographs, mainly concentrating on that time, 1968 to the mid-1980s, when the majority of the structural changes took place. Often, people living today can not identify with the 100-year-old photographs generally published in books similar to this work. So, the first chapter therefore will no doubt ring more than a few bells in people's heads. Thereafter, the chapters are rich with 'people' photographs.

I would like to extend my gratitude not just to the people who provided material but also to Breedon Books and Anton Rippon without whose interest in this project, the book may have not been possible in this particular format. It just leaves me to say, I hope you enjoy the book.

John Alexander
May 2002

Around North

Wilkinson's beverages factory was bombed during World War Two, killing many local people, both young and old. This is a typical Wilkinson 'calling card' for the premise found at 34 King Street, North Shields. By 1983, the former Wilkinson's factory on King Street had been used for many years by builder Clifford Leighton. That year it was sold to Jeffrey Alexander (the author's brother). The date on the deeds is 1877, and with over 100 years having elapsed since then, it was judged that the main building looking out to King

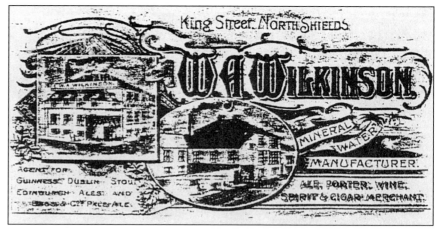

Street and Tynemouth Road would have to be pulled down for safety reasons. This was undertaken 'by hand' as a large scale commercial demolition would have been too costly.

The 60ft-tall Wilkinson's chimney was taken down brick by brick. The pots at the top measured over 3ft in height and weighed heavily.

The second floor was nearly 3ft thick. This massive carpet of concrete was necessary in order to take the weight of the factory horses which were kept upstairs when it was used as Wilkinson's 'pop' factory.

A view from the top of the building at the rear of the yard, the back lane to King Street. The rubble was taken away at a mere cost of £120, and used as 'hard-core' for the Metro Centre shopping complex in Gateshead. The cost in today's terms to remove the equivalent amount of rubble would be in the region of £30,000.

A view from the top of the building that was left standing, looking towards where the law courts now stand.

Stephen Alexander (the author's brother) standing next to his blue Transit van in the yard, in 1994, ten years after both he and Jeffrey had pulled down a vast part of the original structure.

King Street 'yard' in 1994. Standing at the doorway is Stephen, who used the premises to make stained glass windows for the American market.

The Antique & Jewellery Ltd corner shop, situated on Grey Street, North Shields, in 1987.

On the corner of Nile Street, North Shields, in 1972. Shops include the baker Angus Logan, the Co-op, and Fine Fare supermarket.

Jewellers F. Rooney & Sons and Pam's drapery shop, on Wellington Street on a Wednesday afternoon in 1969. Then, it was still commonplace for the majority of high street outlets to obey the unofficial half-day closing rule.

A steam Northern Coal Board train carrying coal along the old track leading up to North Shields railway station, *c.*1910.

In 1979, prior to the Metro system, North Shields railway station platforms looked like this. A simple clue, of course, is there are no overheard power lines.

Another picture of North Shields railway station in 1979, this time taken from another direction on the platform.

The hustle and bustle of Saville Street around 1905. Note the old-style Post Office to the right and not a car in sight, only a lone cyclist occupying the entire road!

On the corner of Saville Street around the year 1928. The well-known name of fashion firm Burton's the tailors was firmly established even then. A game of billiards could be had above the shop.

The now-defunct North Shields Rubber Company, on the corner of Prodhue Street and Marlborough Road, during the mid-1970s.

Thick, horrid, black smoke bellows from the North Shields ferry in 1970, undoubtedly an environmental hazard in its time.

You could buy all your lampshade requirements at Southward Crafts on Grey Street in 1985.

Following in the old traditions, although Pam's drapery shop on Wellington Street suffers a little from graffiti in 1969.

This is a very old version of the Wooden Dolly, *c.*1900. The carvings have a firm place within North Shields folklore and signify the old days of fisherfolk.

The wooden dolly in the 'heart' of North Shields – Northumberland Square to be exact. The image comes from a postcard distributed in around 1968.

A familiar 'Shop at Binn's advertisement on a bus travelling to and from the coast, *c.*1973.

Saville Street, *c.*1962. On the corner is the Home and Colonial store, and next door to that, newsagents H. Wilson.

Looking up Bedford Street, with Littlewoods to the right, *c.*1981.

On the corner of Wellington Street and Church Way, mid-1980s, is the aptly-named Wellington Hotel.

You could buy almost anything at the general dealers, J. Aguiar, on West Percy Road, North Shields, pictured here in 1987. Many local people feel the demise of the corner shop in favour of supermarkets is an unfortunate advancement.

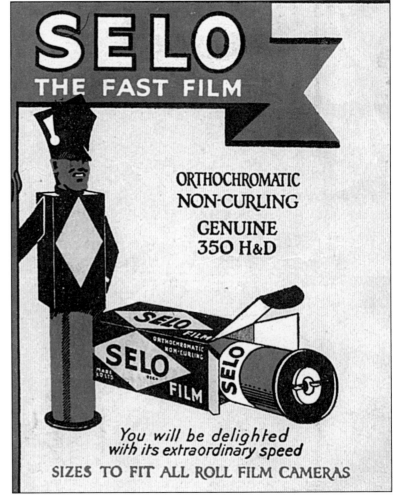

Selo camera film was a popular brand during the 1930s. It was sold in the north, and the simplicity of the advertising image has a childlike quality to it.

Howdon Road, pictured in 1978. Further down the road, near the Christian Aid billboard, there is a small fish and chip shop, beside a bus stop.

A now demolished part of North Shields, pictured here in 1975. In view is the boarded-up Arthur Denham's shoe repairs shop.

The broken windows say it all. Derelict Sarah's Fish Sales closed for business in 1985, and the building was then pulled down.

Senior Electrical Services, 1982. The owners provided more than just electrical goods. They also traded in washing machine spare parts, and belts for vacuum cleaners.

The lack of 'for sale' boards meant that trade was good for shops in Bedford Street during the late 1950s.

Making use of an old building. The popular Central pub on Camden Street in 1997.

These old-style buses, where the passengers would get on at the back, were still in operation towards the end of the 1970s. However, the lack of a rear door was considered rather dangerous if the bus had to make a sudden safety stop.

An advertisement for boys outfitters, Wood & Sons, is plastered on a tram as it travels along Howerd Street in 1929.

Union Street in 1983. The building beside the lamp-post is the old grinding works.

The North Shields Evangelistic Mission, pictured in 1978. It was situated either in Camden Road or Borough Road.

How the North Shields ferry landing looked in April 1972, as seen aboard the ferry on its way to south of the Tyne.

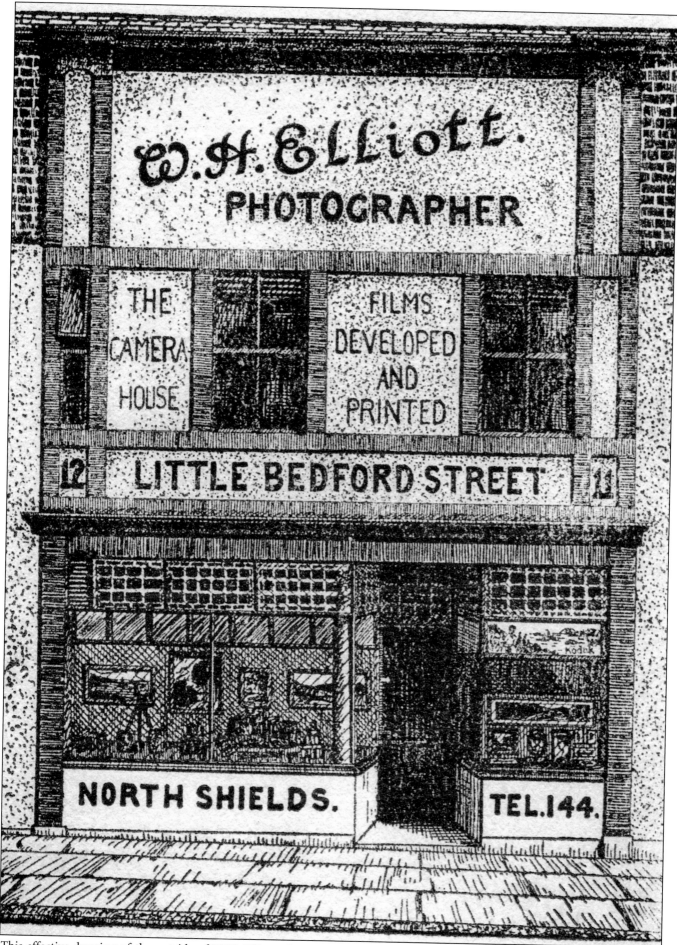

This effective drawing of the outside of W.H. Elliott, photographers, on Little Bedford Street was produced around 1947. The image was on the front of wallets inside of which the negatives were kept.

The battered frontage of the North Shields grinding works, Union Street, in 1984.

The Frank Wappat Memorial Church, opposite a then spare piece of grassy area, pictured 10 years before the now familiar law courts were built.

The North Shields ferry landing, pictured in 1968, the height of 'flower power'.

M. Lowery's shop
on Kensington
Gardens, North
Shields, in 1989.

Atkinson Brothers' fruit and
veg shop Railway Street,
North Shields, in 1984.

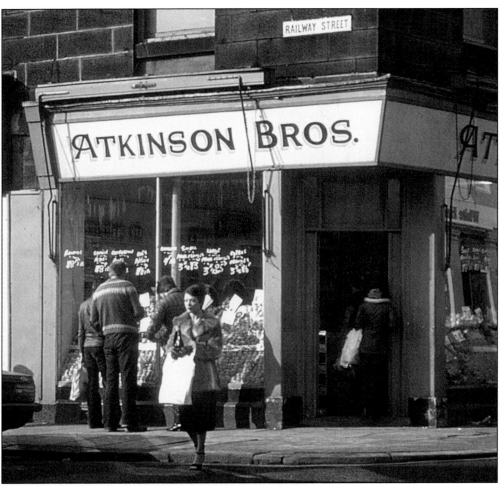

A young girl is startled by the photographer in Duke Street *c*.1918. The advertising posters make interesting reading, namely
forthcoming attractions at Howard Hall (poster on the right).

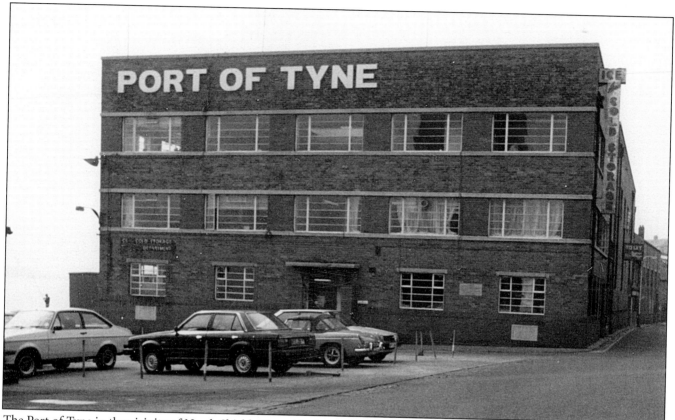

The Port of Tyne in the vicinity of North Shields Quayside, in 1980.

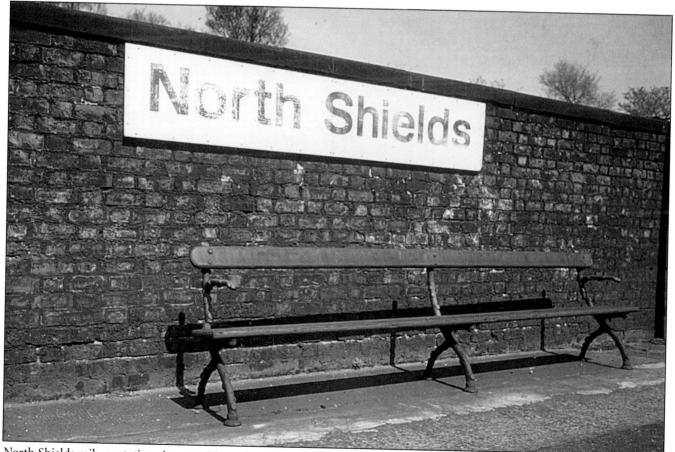

North Shields railway station sign, pre-Metro days. Signs such as this have become collectable.

An old man gathers his thoughts sitting on these steps in North Shields town centre in 1982.

August 1982. The familiar Library Stairs, so much part of the historic past of North Shields. You also have to be fit to climb them!

The Gerard's Furnishing
Company Ltd, Saville
Street, in 1981.

May 1978. The lonely but scenic walkway leading above the Golden Fleece pub, which can be seen to the left of the picture.

Looking out to the Tyne, from a derelict part of North Shields. Photograph taken in 1982.

The terraced properties in Park Crescent, North Shields, in 1981.

Keep your spirits up! No fancy names for this outlet. The off licence of Soden & Sons Ltd, on Collingwood Terrace, in 1974.

Twenty years ago, a North Shields demolition programme lost many curious buildings and old shops. Unfortunately, this bakers was one of them.

A Sunday morning stroll along North Shields quayside, in June 1977, proves to be a breath of fresh air for locals.

Two local lads indulge in a spot of fishing on the quayside in May 1981.

June 1977. The vastness of the River Tyne is seen here in total contrast to the built-up environment of inland.

A massive mountain of ice is used to pack kipper fillets on North Shields quayside in June 1978.

The Berwick Arms public house on Trinity Street in 1992.

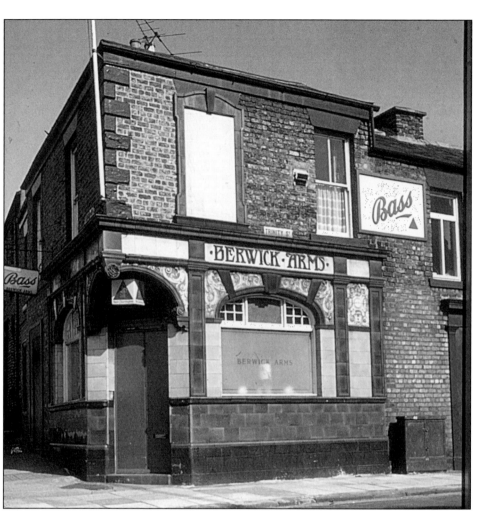

North Shields railway station at the turn of the last century is obviously staging some sort of event, judging by the number of people gathered there.

The main form of 'modern' transport in its day, the coastal tram, *c*.1904. With the price of a ticket being fairly cheap, it's no wonder the top deck is packed.

The Borough Arms public house as it looked in May 1975.

A Tyne and
Wear County
Council plaque
pays respects to
the Old Low
Light, North
Shields.

Another plaque, erected in
1986, on the wall of the old
Stag Line Building, rightly
acknowledges one of
Tyneside's oldest shipping
companies.

The *Leda* arriving in the Tyne for the last time on 8 September 1974.

The *Pride of Walmer* at North Shields in June 1988.

E.E. Sharp & Sons Ltd, on Borough Road, in May 1975.

The big building is that of Smith's Ship Repairers (North Shields) Ltd, Smith's Docks, pictured in June 1987.

Visitors to North Shields could be forgiven for thinking they'd stepped back in time to the Wild West, but no, this wooden structure belongs to the new Royal Quay development in North Shields.

August 2000, and here's another 'unusual' structure found at the Royal Quays, North Shields.

August 1982. In the vicinity of the ferry landing, this run-down property was amusingly taken over by enterprising, nesting birds.

September 1991. This photograph of the Collingwood Mansions was taken from the North Shields ferry.

North Shields Fish Quay area in1978. In view is I. Marshall & Co, fish curers.

Joe Appleby Ltd, North Shields Fish Quay area in 1981.

A Leyland PD2 bus, one of a batch built around 1948 but still in operation until 1969. The vehicle had a front-mounted engine, crash gearbox and an open rear platform for operation by a driver and conductor.

The *Tideflow* setting out on the Tyne in 1963.

An unusual 1983 view of what was then called the Golden Fleece public house, on North Shields quayside. Now it's known as the Porthole.

Hudson Street, 1982. How the popular Wooden Doll pub looked before its renovation.

Everyday Life

A very old postcard showing hard-working North Shields fishwives on the Fish Quay, *c.*1890. If you look closely you can see a policeman hovering around in the background, right of the picture.

A Frazer's work trip to an unknown destination in the early in 1930s provides material for a local photographer.

North Shields ferry landing, passengers getting off the ferry, in April 1972. The children will be around 40 years old now.

A hungry child scoffs on a bag of crisps. Just one of a few passengers on the North Shields ferry, again in April 1972.

Two children fishing by North Shields quayside, in 1980.

Two happy bridesmaids at the wedding of North Shields resident Jean Lines in 1962. The blonde girl is Beryl Drydon who emigrated to Australia.

Mr and Mrs
Edwards, pictured in
the back yard of
their home in
Addison Street,
North Shields, 60
years ago.

Formica workers scale the lofty heights of scaffolding in North Shields during the early 1960s.

Bridesmaids Audrey Caisley and Margaret Galbraith, are in flowery mood at the wedding of Pamela Margaret Howerd (née Dodds) in November 1966.

Smiles from the newly-weds – Pamela and her husband, Anthony James Howerd, who originated from London.

Bulk Carrier Fleet

| M.V. Gloxinia | 10340 dwt. 1958 | M.V. Ixia | 26140 dwt. 1964 |
| M.V. Photinia | 10350 dwt. 1961 | M.V. Zinnia | 26603 dwt. 1968 |

STAG LINE, LIMITED

1 HOWARD STREET, NORTH SHIELDS, NORTHUMBERLAND
Telephone North Shields 70435

We are building up a team of established Seafarers who wish to make a career with a local company which provides a close link with the family at home.

Each summer we have a limited number of Deck and Engineer Officer Cadet vacancies for school leavers of 16/18 years of age who hope to obtain four G.C.E. "O" level passes including Maths, Physics (or allied subject) and English. We also have openings for Deck Boys and Engine Room Boys from School leavers who only obtain one "O" level pass or a high grade C.S.E. in Maths or Physics but still wish to work for their Navigating and Engineer Officer Certificates.

A 1972 advertisement for school-leavers to join seafaring company, Stag Line Ltd, 1 Howard Street, North Shields. Vacancies were for deck and engineering officer cadets. They were open to 16–18-year-olds with the appropriate 'O' level passes.

Take your partners, please for a spot of ballroom dancing in June 1969 at the North Shields Masonic Ballroom.

Choirboys make their way to church in an orderly fashion, *c.*1974.

Born in North Shields, Sally Moody later moved to Canada. Her Aunt Ames had this photograph turned into a postcard in 1921 and sent out to various relatives.

December 1966 and a student proudly reclines in the 'chair for the future', which was designed by James Stephenson and Dennis Hodges. The chair was made locally in a workshop and sold exclusively in a furniture store in Park View, Whitley Bay.

Frank Nettleton (the author's late uncle, 1936–2002) aged 15 in 1951, pictured during a work break. The girls either side of him are unknown, but he's quite clearly enjoying the attention!

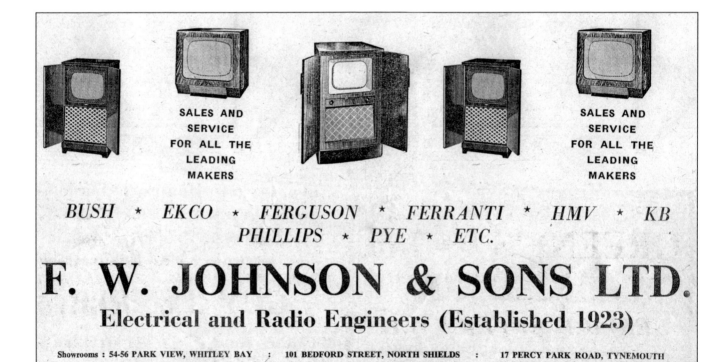

SALES AND SERVICE FOR ALL THE LEADING MAKERS

SALES AND SERVICE FOR ALL THE LEADING MAKERS

BUSH ★ EKCO ★ FERGUSON ★ FERRANTI ★ HMV ★ KB
PHILLIPS ★ PYE ★ ETC.

F. W. JOHNSON & SONS LTD.
Electrical and Radio Engineers (Established 1923)

Showrooms : 54-56 PARK VIEW, WHITLEY BAY : 101 BEDFORD STREET, NORTH SHIELDS : 17 PERCY PARK ROAD, TYNEMOUTH
Office and Works : 58-60 HOTSPUR STREET, TYNEMOUTH ——— PHONE NOS. : NORTH SHIELDS 1431-2 and WHITLEY BAY 21582

Television sets for sale at F.W. Johnson & Sons Ltd. Advertisement from the *Whitley Bay Guardian* in 1956.

A splendid advertisement taken from a 1966 edition of the *Whitley Bay Guardian*. It shows the 'marvellous' new Hoover washing machine which could have been purchased for the princely sum of £35 from F.W. Johnson & Sons Ltd. They had outlets scattered throughout the coast, including 10 Union Quay, North Shields. The product boasted many fine technological advances, including a large wringer that could easily take a full sized blanket.

Senior citizens in good spirits at an OAPs' Christmas knees-up at the Albion Assembly Rooms in 1957.

Mrs Mary Knox, from Coronation Street, pictured here at a local photographers in 1918.

A young boy finds comfort with his pet dog in an a now demolished area now known as Meadowell Housing Estate, *c.*1948.

Rude awakening. North Shields quayside, and two young children prepare a tin bath for their pet dog taking a nap in the bottom left of the photograph.

A World War One family picture, showing a soldier, his wife and their little boy. From left to right are Barbara, Norman and John Thirlwell.

Two North Shields fishwives are hard at work at the quayside *c.*1900.

North Shields resident Kitty
Dawson, pictured in 1911.
Possibly photographed by
Bernard Jarvis.

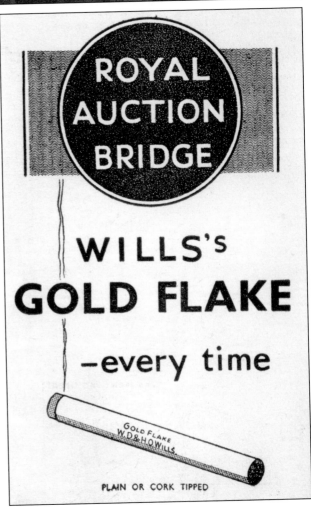

A local collector of old posters recounts this one for Wills Gold
Flake cigarettes having pride of place outside a local North Shields
newsagents. It's probably dated early to mid-1960s.

Pretty as peaches. Sixties bridesmaids are (left to right) P. Osbourne, H. Roberts, S. Gallacher, at a wedding in 1965.

This advertisement from a December 1966 edition of the *Whitley Bay Guardian* proudly separates the men from the boys who were directed to buy 'Man Style' clothing from Shephard's of North Shields. Shephard's was situated in Bedford Street.

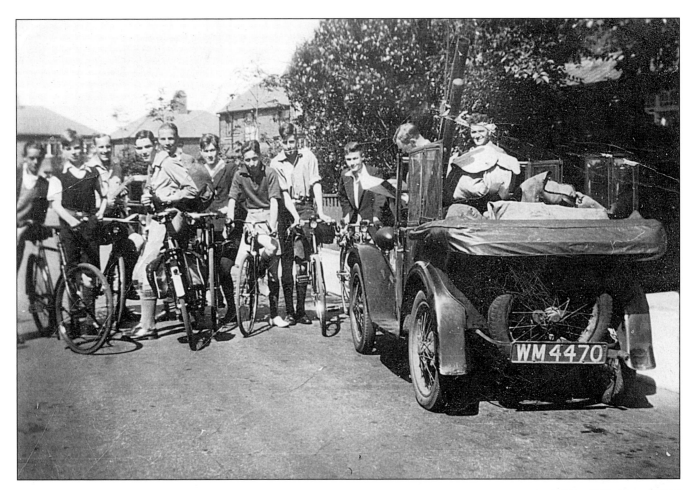

Scotland-born Cameron McDonald was involved in these regular keep-fit bike rides involving young lads from the area. 'It was good disciple,' recalls Cameron.

This picture of a gentleman standing next to a bicycle decorated with Union flags was donated by a local resident. The problem was, it only existed in the form of a damaged negative that had faded badly over the years. However, with the help of advanced computerised digital manipulation methods, it has been successfully repaired. The picture is probably something to do with the celebration of Empire Day, *c.*1930.

At the time when this photograph was snapped, at a local photographer's in 1932, American movie actor, George Raft, was a big star. As today, popular dress modes cross the Atlantic and this chap looks clearly influenced by them.

The Reliant three-wheel car had not become the brunt of jokes when this advertisement from the *Whitley Bay Guardian* was published in 1973. Nor had it been associated with the comedy drama, *Only Fools and Horses*. Car dealer, A.B. Firmin, on Waterville Road, North Shields, sold the Reliant vehicle. And just look at what you got. Tyres lasting on average 40,000 miles, and a rustless fibreglass body. An absolute bargain for the low budget road user.

SAVE
WITH
RELIANT

Save on . . .

★ Tyres - average 40,000 miles
★ Petrol - up to 65 m.p.g.
★ Road tax - only £10
★ Body repairs - rustless fibreglass

— and a Reliant can be driven on a motor cycle licence!

ORDER YOUR NEW MODEL
NOW FOR 1973 — AND
BEAT V.A.T.

A. B. FIRMIN
RELIANT MAIN DEALERS

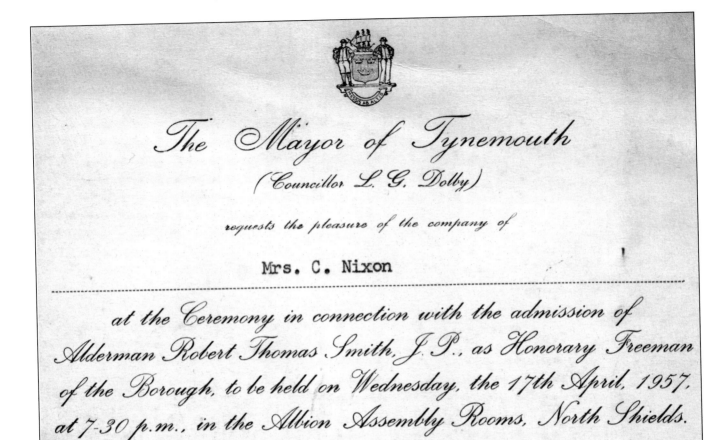

The Mayor of Tynemouth, Councillor L.G. Dolby, sent this invitation to a Mrs Nixon, to attend the ceremony in connection with the admission of Alderman Robert Thomas Smith, JP, as Honorary Freeman of the Borough. The event was held on Wednesday 17 April 1957, in the Albion Assembly Rooms. North Shields.

Bar staff at a North Shields pub, *c.*1956. Pictured from left to right are Winnie Kerr, unknown, Aggie Adie, unknown.

A Sunday School day trip outing in 1938. The outbreak of World War Two was only 12 months away. Such easy-going family breaks would become a rarity.

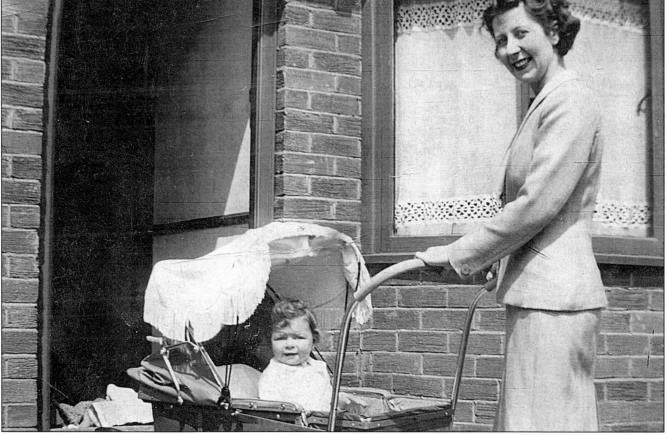

A smartly-dressed Mrs Scales pictured with her baby daughter, Patricia, *c.*1943. Mr Scales was away fighting in the war when the photograph was taken.

A rare picture of the towering figure of Roland Park (right), who became famous as the most active photographer of his generation in the North-East. He snapped everything from aerial shots (hence the aeroplane), fishwives, streets and buildings. He was also believed to have been a school friend of Stan Laurel, one half of comedy duo Laurel and Hardy.

Pictured in the North Shields Crescent Club, late-1950s. Left to right: unknown, Sid Kerr, Winnie Kerr, Phoebe Frazer.

Right to left, brothers Derek and Sid Kerr Snr are photographed beside their pet dog in 1961.

A delightful poster for Be-Ro flour, mid-1930s, was retrieved from North Shields railway station and has since been kept in a local man's collection.

North Shields' beach area, around 1962. In view is the famous Knott's Flats, named after Sir James Knott.

A Saturday morning, outside Woolworth's store on Saville Street, 1980. A boy waits on his 'chopper' style bike, probably for a friend to turn up.

The familiar image of the fruit and veg stall just next to Woolworth's, in 1980.

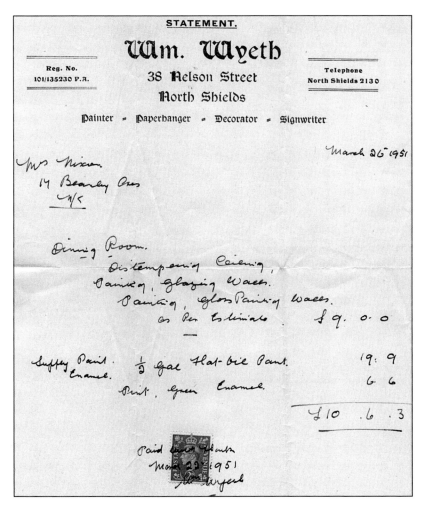

W. Wyeth's decorator's receipt, dated March 1951. The cost of painting and decorating a dining room came to just over £10. Judge for yourself, was that a reasonable price 50 years ago?

John Alexander Snr (the author's grandfather) won many cups for bowls from 1920 to 1936. He was often regional champion.

During the 1930s, regular meetings were held in North Shields and Whitley Bay, by the Society of Pitman's Certificated teachers of Shorthand. Their conferences attracted many people from all over the country. This is John Woodhead, chairman of the Pitman Executive Council.

J.S. Whitfield was chairman of the North-Eastern District branch of the Pitman Society.

Louis James was a Pitman conference secretary. He was in charge of booking the venues and organising the appropriate hotels for guests.

W.L. Dowling was chairman of the Pitman Reception Committee. He is photographed here in 1931 by Gladstone Adams of Whitley Bay.

James Hynes held the senior position, that of president of the Society of Pitman's Certificated Teachers of Shorthand.

Librarian Janet Dare reads a story to a group of enthusiastic young children in 1973. Sitting on Janet's lap is Zoe Humphries, with John and Susan Dive close by.

Two military men stationed at Marden Farm during World War One, share a joke.

North Shields Fish Quay, *c.*1907. Three young children delight in a ride on a fish cart.

William Laverick started trading under the name, Laverick's Cycles in 1900. William moved to Whitley Bay in the 1920s where he opened various shops. His son, Angus (pictured on the right), followed in his father Bob's footsteps by opening up the shop in Cullercoats, North Shields. Bob is seen here with his wife, Peggy, and son, Angus.

Laverick's shop in John Street, Cullercoats, North Shields, during the mid-1950s. The bicycle in view belonged to a local butcher who had stopped by at the shop to buy a pump.

Laverick's in the early 1960s. In the window is the new Raleigh RSW 16 cycle which could be bought for £29.

Bob and Peggy Laverick pictured outside the Cullercoats' premise in 1963. On leaving school, Bob started work as a signwriter. He later used his expertise to undertake the signwriting above his own shop.

A three-year-old Angus Laverick, pictured on an old style child's trike, *c.*1950.

A group of hard-working North Shields fishwives gather together, pictured at the quayside, in the early 1930s.

Christmas 1966, and local children set up 'store' to help raise money for charity. Pictured from left to right are Carole Fitzgerald, Claire Whitfield and Lucy Metcalfe.

The sun has got its hat on. The wedding of Julie Cliffe to Graham Dumphy at Holy Saviour's Church, Tynemouth, in 1973, brings out the 'hip' sartorial elegance of bride, groom and guests.

Tea up! A family take refreshment in a specially provided tent on Tynemouth sands in 1935.

The Co-operative Society has been present in North Shields since 1860. What started off as a little barque 142 years ago has grown into the success it is today. Despite the introduction of massive shopping centres, the smaller localised Co-op stores still have thousands of loyal customers.

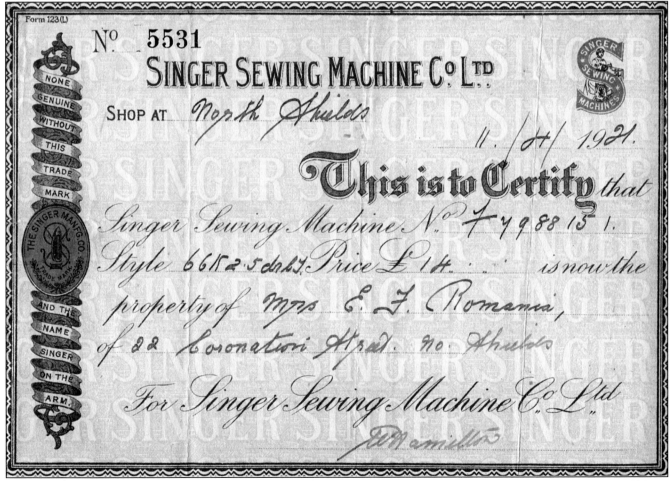

A proof of purchase guarantee slip for a Singer sewing machine, sold to a Mrs Romania, of Coronation Street, North Shields, in April 1921. The price, a costly £14!

Four young ladies have their picture taken on the wooden steps of an old tea room on Tynemouth sands in 1933. Perhaps you recognise a face or two?

Behind Stanley Street West, *c.*1905. A married couple proudly show off their young baby.

Tynemouth Sands' old-style wooden tea rooms have been rarely seen close up. Unfortunately, the proprietor's surname has been covered by items hanging from the hut.

At the back of this photograph are the words, 'Summer school holidays, 1936'. The image was obtained from a negative found amongst some bric-a-brac.

Northern Gas are replacing mains

"Here's the way that it affects you"

Local man Sid Kerr has provided numerous photographs in this book. A entertainer and actor, this is one of his many appearances in a 1984 advertisement for British Gas which had pride of place in the North Shields Gas showroom.

A group of elderly North Shields fishwives pictured here in 1937. The photograph was taken in the vicinity of the Fish Quay.

Friends enjoy a few drinks in the Salutation pub, Front Street, Tynemouth, in 1961. One of the North-East's favourite tipples, a bottle of brown ale, can be seen on the table.

North Shields trawlermen. Pictured in the middle is James Corby Patterson, *c.*1932.

On the Tynemouth beach in 1931. One of the notices behind refers to a swimming gala which took place on Saturday 8 August 1931, in Tynemouth's open-air bathing pool.

Three young men at the local technical college in 1964. The man on the right is Ritchie Rutherford.

A wedding buffet takes place in the North Eastern pub in West Percy Street, North Shields, in 1950.

A register wedding in North Shields in the mid-1950s. The man on the right is Arnold Robson.

Tynemouth amateur swimming club, 1982. The gentleman is Councillor Ron Oliver. On the right is Catherine Wrigley (née Lines).

Tynemouth amateur swimming club, *c.*1982.

Katherine Simmons, third from the left, was born and grew up in the area. She later moved to the south. Here she is as a 16-year-old, pictured with friends in the 1940s.

Eva Alexander (née Nettleton, the author's mother, pictured centre) with two friends on a trip to the coast in 1948.

A group of people enjoying a day trip in the countryside in 1935. They were members of North Shields Cycle Club.

The café, facing the Plaza, in Tynemouth, pictured during the mid-1930s. This photograph was obtained from a negative bought at a car boot sale.

A general dealer's store in Union Street around 1933. Beamish Museum would have a field day collecting the memoriabila found in that shop alone!

A receipt dated
August 1935, from
William Hunter,
grocer and baker,
whose shop was
situated in
Stephenson Street,
North Shields.

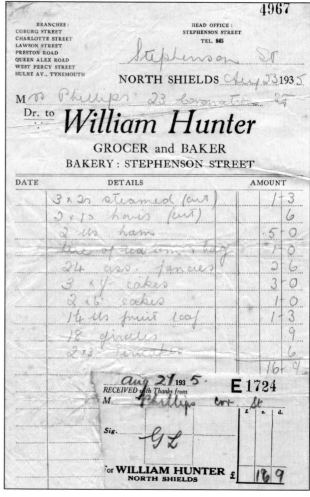

Christmas 1966, and wide-eyed, five-year-old Raymond Smith opens a local Christmas fair while the Revd L. Paulin looks on.

North Shields gas works around the turn of the last century. Pictured second from right is Mr Turnbull, whose family still live in and around North Shields.

Famous Tynemouth lifeboatman James Blackburn, pictured *c.*1912. A grand old man of the sea, James lived to the ripe old age of 94.

Muscle bound. A group of young men on Tynemouth sands in 1964. Pictured from left to right are: Ritchie Rutherford, unknown, Brian Curlie, unknown, Norman Hardwick.

Office employees at Welch's sweet factory in Norham Road, North Shields, 1956, get ready for a works trip to Alnwick. Welch's also had premises in Whitley Bay.

Not seen since the Land Girls of World War Two: Bertha Rutherford strikes a stance for women's lib. She became a lady van driver for Frazer's in the early 1950s.

Children enjoy the Queen's silver jubilee celebrations of 1977. The party was held at the Cannon Inn, on the Coast Road, North Shields.

Specially designed for the younger children. Another part of the Cannon Inn provides 1977 jubilee entertainment, balloons, refreshment and food, for the excited children, many of them pre-school, but now in their early 30s.

Have you ever seen a truck more laden with crates than this in the picture of Frazer's of North Shields during the late 1930s? It's quite amazing how it managed to move, never mind reach its destination!

That's

The hugely popular BBC drama *When The Boat Comes In* was shot on location in all parts of the North-East, but the programme makers came back to North Shields time and time again. This photograph was taken in 1976 and shows local actor Sid Kerr (centre, and the owner of the following TV photographs). The next 13 pictures show various scenes and the actors and actresses involved.

When The Boat Comes In was a series of 51, 50-minute programmes, made during the years 1975–7/81. The creator was James Mitchell and the memorable theme song was performed by the late Alex Glasgow.

Something normally (but not necessarily) kept out of camera shot, the boom mike is moved into place. The actor on the right is local comedian Bobby Pattinson, who is still a regular on the northern club circuit.

Setting the scene in Coronation Street (now pulled down), North Shields. These fake old lamps managed to create the 1920s feel to the programme.

James Bolam and another cast member chat together during a break in filming. James is best known for his role in *Whatever Happened to the Likley Lads?* and other comedy shows like *Only When I Laugh.*

James Bolam and another cast member rehearse for a fight scene while lighting technicians go about their work in the background, seemingly totally disinterested in what is going on.

North Shields provided many historical locations, without much effort on the part of the programme makers, to give the town that 1930s' feel.

A *When the Boat Comes In* crowd scene in Howard Street, North Shields. The actress second from the right is Susan Jameson, who first found fame in 1969 in the television series, *Take Three Girls*, a tale about students living life together in a flat in London.

The extras you see here were invariably drawn from the North-East club circuit. Bobby Pattinson, Sid Kerr, and Alan Snell were but a few.

Two cameramen set up the screen angles for a scene shot in the vicinity of Coronation Street, North Shields.

An interesting story surrounds this picture. Lorna Workman – the girl pictured here – was a local reporter sent down to cover the story of the BBC filming. She expressed an interest in being an extra and was immediately taken aside and given a costume. Minutes later, she was in front of the cameras!

Susan Jameson's character is in electioneering mood for a scene shot in King Street, North Shields, in the vicinity of the old Wilkinson's pop factory. Susan played Myra Booth in *Coronation Street*, from 1963–8.

Much of the *Where the Boat Comes In* locations have now vanished in the wake of a demolition scheme.

In *When the Boat Comes In*, James Bolam played Jack Ford, who had come home to Gallowshields on Tyneside after the end of World War One to finds an area depressed and full of unemployment, falling in with the Seaton family. The series followed Ford's determined effort to make his mark on the world.

North Shields FC's ground was used for this *SuperGran* scene involving fictitious rival teams. Local children were drafted in as extras. They did not have to be members of Equity, the actors' union, as long as they did not speak.

An amusing scene involved actors wearing comical 'Bobby Charlton' style comb-over hairstyle wigs.

Comic acting talent Roy Kinnear sadly died on a film set, five years after this photograph was taken in North Shields football ground.

SuperGran Gudrun Ure and soccer great George Best try to pretend the summer sunshine is above, but in fact a cold winter wind was blowing.

Phoar, it's cold! *SuperGran* actress Gudrun Ure has to put on her coat as the cold north-east wind blows. Gunrun's character was a 'wrinkly' with back pain one day, then the next she was transformed from a quivering old wreck into a granny with super powers. Her mission was to rid the town of crime.

In the dugout, soccer star George Best turns his hand to acting, alongside Ian Towel, who played Willard.

Not only did the beer taste nice, but the crates come in handy too! A football scene is shot in late afternoon, just as the natural light is fading.

Scots-born actor Iain
Cuthbertson as
Scunner Campbell,
and Lee Marshall,
who played Scunner's
nephew in the series.

In between takes, Iain Cuthbertson paces himself for the next scene. Iain is best known for his roles in the movie *The Railway Children* (1970) and TV shows, *Budgie* and *Sutherland's Law*.

A scene from *The Black Candle* shot in North Shields in 1991. *The Black Candle* was dramatised from a novel by the late Dame Catherine Cookson (1906-98) and screened on ITV.

'Eeeee, gizza cuddle, pet!' Actors participating in the 1984 children's TV series, *Dramarama*. The programme was made by Tyne Tees TV. There were six half-hour episodes, mainly involving a mixture of mystery and suspense. One such title was *The Universe Downstairs*.

The *Dramarama* film crew pinned a 'police' sign outside this school in North Shields, proving the point that things are not all they seem in television land!

BBC Radio Newcastle presenter Frank Wappat's long association with the Memorial Church in North Shields in an interesting one. The following pictures tell the potted story. Here Frank is pictured with 1980s Italian tenor Renato. Frank 'discovered' him at the Memorial Church. The tenor also recorded songs with Renee and they went onto score a number-one hit in the pop charts, with *Save My Love*. An amusing story surrounds this meeting between Frank and Renato. Afterwards, the pair went for a drink at the Locomotive pub. Funnily enough, no one knew who Renato was, even though he was, at the time, one of the biggest names in British pop music. As Frank said, 'Well, you don't expect a chart-topper to be drinking in your local.'

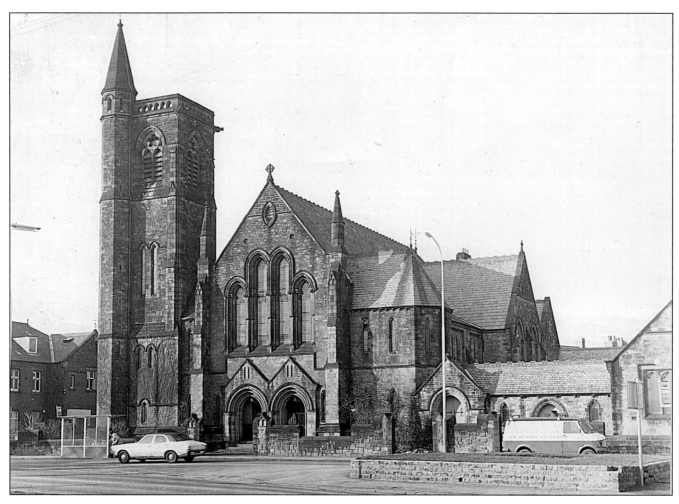

How the Memorial Church looked in 1980, before Frank started its renovation. It was a derelict building with no railings nor gates. Frank, with the help of friends and radio listeners, set about putting things to right.

Restoring the derelict property was Frank's first concern. It cost over £150,000. That's a lot of money now, but it was even more then. Frank raised every penny, working day and night, raising money with dances, cabarets, after-dinner speeches, general talks and discos.

This picture shows the restored church late at night, lit by the floodlights. Unfortunately, two weeks after the photograph was taken, vandals smashed all the floodlights. A listener to Frank's radio show paid for replacement lights. They lasted one week before they too were destroyed by vandals.

Frank Wappat, pictured with the famous Irish tenor Cavan O'Connor, and Cavan's wife, Rita Teyte, who is the niece of Dame Maggie Teyte, the legendary soprano. The trio met up in 1986 at a gathering to celebrate the restoration of the church.

In good voice. Frank leads the church's choir at a centenary service.

From the first day Frank reopened the church, the queues for Sunday service would invariably stretch all the way down the road, such was the popularity of Frank's radio show.

The magnificent pipe organ did not function when Frank took over. He had to restore it to its pristine glory and put the beautiful sounds onto CD and cassette.

A typical Sunday service with a staggering 1,000 local people in the church at one time.

All ears. Cavan O'Connor listens intently to the radio broadcast reel-to-reel recording at the Memorial Church in 1984.

On top of the world. Frank does a sponsored climb to the top of the tower as a mark of celebration of the Memorial Church.

The North Shields Fish Quay Festival began in the mid-1980s and has grown to be a major attraction. It is still run every year and not only manages to draw vast crowds, but also entertainers worldwide have appeared there.

Just what is in those big
buckets? It's not sure
whether this gentleman
is a local fisherman or a
charity worker at the
Fish Quay Festival in
1989.

The North Shields Fish Quay Festival in 1989. Since its birth, it remains Europe's biggest free open music event.

North Shields' famous adopted 'son' Arthur Stanley Jefferson (1890–1965), otherwise known as comedy actor, Stan Laurel, who along with partner Oliver Hardy, formed one of the funniest duos in movies. Stan lived most of his childhood in North Shields where his father was involved with local theatre. Determined to make it big in what were then 'silent' films, Stan left for America. This is one of his earliest 'publicity' photographs during the early years in the United States, c.1919.

Stan Laurel, c.1926. Stan never forgot his Geordie roots and made visits to North Shields and the rest of the UK, with comedy partner and friend Oliver Hardy. They'd often entertain the British fans by performing memorable scenes from their movies. They must have been a sight in the flesh, for Oliver was a towering 6ft 4ins tall, while Stan was 6ft.

Making it big. By 1927, Stan Laurel had established himself as one of the rising comedy stars in America. His heroes included Charlie Chaplin and the Keystone Cops. This drawing was traced from a photograph; it dates from around 1927.

Stan Laurel's monument, in Laurel Court, North Shields, was erected in memory of the man in the 1990s, a somewhat delayed reaction considering the world-famous funnyman died in 1965. Nevertheless, it is a fine compliment to an 'adopted' Geordie and his achievements on a global stage.

Stan Laurel and Oliver Hardy, on a visit to Britain in1952. Their last movie together was *Atoll K* (aka *Robinson Crusoeland*) made in 1950, when Stan was 60 and Oliver 58. At the time, it wasn't considered one of their best works, but today, although it still has its critics, the general consensus is that it is quite a nice little film, with some funny and clever moments. It is not known whether or not it was ever screened on British TV, although it is available to buy on video.

Oliver Hardy's jovial features take pride of place, below the statue, alongside his comic partner, Stan Laurel. The moulds appear to have taken the brunt of the north-east wind blowing in from the Tyne, or maybe they have been victims of vandalism. Perhaps it would have been a better idea to cast them in bronze as opposed to concrete.

Laurel Court in 2002, a regenerated area which was much neglected during the 1970s. The new housing breathed fresh air into what had become a depressing part of North Shields. The views from the houses look out along the mouth of the Tyne and the Quayside.

Tynemouth Priory Theatre, in Percy Street. The theatre has occupied the building – a former church – since 1973. The following images show a selection of productions throughout the years, starting with the 'Swinging Sixties'.

Tynemouth Priory Theatre Season, 1966–7, a production of *An Ideal Husband* by Oscar Wilde, directed by Ria Thompson. Pictured from left right are Joan Corbitt (maid), Claire Bailey (Mrs Cheveley), Audrey Nicol (Lady Markby), Robert Bradshaw (Sir Robert Chiltern), Irene Ridley (Lady Chiltern).

Season 1971–2, a production of *My Three Angels* by Sam and Bella Spewack. Back row, pictured from left to right: Joan Corbitt (Madame Parole), Tony Hurst (Paul Cassagon), Christopher Carr (Sub Lieutenant Espoir). Front row: Eileen Armstrong (Emilie Dulay), Christine Coaster (Marie Louse Dulay).

Season 1979–80, a production of *The Pied Piper,* book, music and lyrics by Bob Jeffrey and Roger Burgess. Directed by Belle Holmes and performed by members of the Tynemouth Priory Youth Group.

Season 1980–1, a production of *Hay Fever* by Noel Coward. Directed by Ian Henry. Back row from left to right: Roland Coaster (Sandy), Alan McKinlay (Simon), Sheila Hudson (Clara), Steve Arnott (David). Middle row: Judith Stephenson (Jackie), Lorraine Rudd (Myra). Front row unknown.

Season 1984–5, *The Wizard of Oz* directed by Steve Arnott. From left to right: Eric Peel (The Scarecrow), Leigh Henry (Dorothy), Paul Jennings (The Tin Man), Ian Henry (The Cowardly Lion).

Season 1988–9, *Ring Round The Moon* by Jean Anouilh, directed by Elsie Dixon. Back row, from left to right: Alan McKinlay, John Gray, Norman Ord. Middle row: Maurice Egan, Irene Pollington, Julia Elliot, John Cox. Front row: Val Whittingham, Rosaline Robinson, Tanya Young Pam Cowey.

Season 1996–7, *Cabaret*. Music by John Kander. Lyrics by Fred Ebb from the book by Joe Masteroff. Directed by Chris Carr. Back row, from left to right: Neville Wanless (Herr Schultz), Michael Harrison (Emcee), David Cosgrove (Clifford Bradshaw). Front: Marsha Mckinlay.

Season 1999–2000. *The Dairy of Anne Frank* by Frances Goodrich and Albert Hackett. Directed by Marsha McKinlay. Steve Mobbs (Mr Frank). Ladies from left to right: Claire Thompson (Anne), Cathy Scott (Mrs Frank), Amy Telford (Margot Frank).

Season 1999–2000, *Blood Brothers* by Willy Russell, directed by Audrey Morrow. From left to right: Tanya Young (Linda), Brendan Egan and Paul Hencher (The Twins, Mickey and Eddy).

Season, 2000–1, *Katherine Howard*, directed by Audrey Morrow. Colin Lostings (King Henry), Tanya Young (Katherine).

The Rex Cinema on Billy Mill Avenue was opened on 8 December 1936 and demolished 60 years later in September 1996. During its heyday it screened movies like the 1946 classic *Brief Encounter*, starring Trevor Howard and Celia Johnson. During the 1950s, it was a place to be for courting teenage couples.

Nothing left but rubble. The North-Eastern Co-op successfully acquired the right to build a £580,000 funeral parlour on the old Rex Cinema site. The man in the funeral garb is Norman Dowson.

Young members of the Gillian Quinn School of Dancing prepare for a production of the musical, *Salad Days*, which was staged at the Plaza Repertory Theatre, Christmas 1966. At the piano is John Reay.

Smiles all round for the cast members of *Salad Days*. Leading the adult cast list was Denise Bainbridge.

Don't let your eyes deceive you. This isn't a Victorian photograph, but a 1960s amateur production of the curious tale of *Pink String and Sealing Wax*. From left to right are Cyril Bairstow, Linda Dorrity, Carol Foulkes, Brian Dixon.

In this high-tech world of pocket-sized digital camcorders, DVD players and Super VHS, it really is intriguing to think today that having a 'home' projector, cine-camera, or having access to one such 'mod con' in the mid-1960s, you'd be considered the envy of your friends and family. Members of the Cine-Tape Society gather for their annual film-making competition. From left to right are J.R. Wrightson, Florence Richards, Don Luck, George Riley.

August 1973. Sisters Judith and Denise Kelly attend a stunning art exhibition by grammar school boy Martin Edge. Martin's talents came to light following his winning a book cover illustration competition. But where is he now?

'Oh, how spiffing, old boy!' Members of a local theatre group in character for a 1930s production of *Oh Lady, Lady* by P.J. Wodehouse.

This poster for the horror movie *Man-Made Monster* might bring back 'scary' memories to film fans of the year 1941 at the Rex Cinema, North Shields. Horror movies did badly during the war years because nothing was more real or more horrific than war itself.

Popular actress Denise Welch was brought up in North Shields. Her father had Welch's sweet factory in the neighbouring town of Whitley Bay. She is best known for parts in *Soldier, Soldier* and *Coronation Street*.

North Shields, during the late 1920s. A giant poster advertising a coming movie feature starring American star Harold Lloyd (1893–1971). Harold's career slumped when filmgoers heard his voice following the introduction of talkies. It was considered his speech never matched his silent screen persona.

Two boys from King's School prepare for a drama production of *Robin Hood* in 1937. The smaller boy clearly couldn't wait to get into costume.

A *News Guardian* advertisement for the Albion Cinema, North Shields, in January 1973. Then showing were Walt Disney's *The Aristocats* and *My Dog, The Thief.*

ALBION
CINEMA

NORTH SHIELDS. Telephone 73404

Monday, January 1, 1973 — for 6 days
Cont. daily Mon. to Fri. 1.45 p.m.
Cont. Saturday 4.35 p.m.
Walt Disney presents

THE
ARISTOCATS
(U) Technicolor
Mon. to Fri. 3.15 6.05 8.55
Saturday 6.05 and 8.55

ALSO

MY DOG, THE THIEF
(U) Technicolor
Mon. to Fri. 1.55 4.45 7.35
Saturday at 4.45 7.35
Last complete show at 7.35 p.m.

Children's Matinee Saturday at 1.30

All Cartoon Show

Giant children's toys come to life at King Edward Primary's School's Christmas Fayre, in 1997. The characters are all, of course, from the *Wizard of Oz.*

Schooldays

Linskill Secondary School, January 1955. Back row: Ian Hope, Dave Patterson, Joseph Thompson, John Norris, Brian Stephenson, Dave Percy, Ritchie Rutherford. Front row: unknown, Brian West, Jackie Oliver, 'Pepper' Hargreaves (headmaster), Tony Dodds, Reggie Collins, Eddie Scott.

Western Board School, 1951. Brian Purves, Alfie Smith, Noel Currie, Tommy Herbertson, Nelson Grey, Brian Ritches, Philip Dixon, Derek Fagin, Ritchie Rutherford. Middle row: Mr Smith (teacher), Tommy Donaghoe, Cyril Nicholson, Brian Stephenson, Joseph Thompson, Brian Kent, Lance Carr, Dave Percy, Dixon Crova, Tony Cervantes. Front row: Raymond Smith, Jackie Gilbert, John Gilespie, Albert Cummins, Norman Hill, Brian Chater, Bob Latimer, Eddie Storrer, Eddie Walker, Ronnie Richardson.

Ralph Gardener School, 1959. Back row (left to right): unknown, Paul Burton, Billy Daniels, John Carr,Ronnie Hoye, Eric Bullcraig, unknown Middle row: Peter Errington, unknown, Alex Latimer, Ray George, unknown, Sid Kerr, Harry Wilson, Alan Percy, unknown, Ray Wright, Dennis Kerringan, Dave Downie. Front row: Billy Reed, unknown, Alan Taylor, unknown, Billy Monaghan, (Teacher Mr Foster), unknown, Ian Hall, unknown, Derek, Porter, unknown.

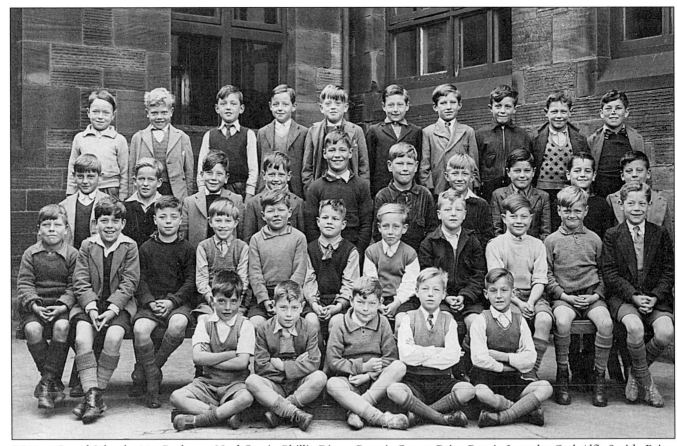

Western Board School, 1951. Back row: Noel Currie, Phillip Dixon, Ronnie Crowe, Brian Purvis, Lancelot Carl, Alfie Smith, Brian Stephenson, Tommy Sharp, Michael Golightly, Eddie Storer. Second row down: Cyril Nicholson, Tommy Herbertson, Jimmy Bell, Colin Davidson, Tony Cervantes, Edward McGough, Derek Fagin, Terry Fisher, Tommy Donaghoe, Dave Percy. Second row up: Brian Chater, Norman Hill, Victor Johnson, Billy Henderson, Jimmy White. Billy New, Brian Yelland, Brian Smith, Alan Vogel, Brian Riches, Scotty Thompson. Front row: Jimmy Errington, Spadge Brown, Ritchie Rutherford, George Houghton, Jimmy Isbister.

Western Board School 1951. Back row: Mr Kershaw (teacher), John Gillesphie, Billy Henderson, Jackie Gilbert, Ritchie Rutherford, Noel Currie, Victor Johnson, Brian Ritches, Alan Voger, Lance Carr. Phillip Dixon, Alfie Smith, Derek Fagin. Middle row: Colin Davidson, Tommy Donaghoe, Brian Stephenson, Scotty Thompson, Dave Percy, Tommy Sharp, Tommy Henderson, Brian Purvis, Cyril Nicholson. Front row: George Brown, Norman Hill, Brian Chater, George Houghton, Jimmy White, Eddie Storer, Jimmy Eprington, Billy New, Brian Yelland.

Children from Priory School celebrate the now-forgotten Empire Day. Some are dressed in their Scout and Cub uniforms whilst others have opted for more decorative clothing. A Union flag is draped behind them.

Pupils adhere strictly to the school rules and sit with their back rigidly upright at Trinity School around the year 1904. The female teacher, wearing a less than feminine tie, looks unusual to say the least.

Western School in 1906. Second row from the front, second from left is Thomasina Edwards who sadly died at the age of 23. Her relatives still live in North Shields.

Western School, 1922. Second row from the front, the first pupil on the left is James Corby Patterson.

Spring Gardens School, 1949. Pictured from left to right, back row: Unknown, John Cooper, unknown, Tom Ranshaw, Harry Davy, unknown, headmaster Mr Turnbull. Second row down: unknown, unknown, Alan Redhead, Derek Harper. Second row up: Maureen Wrathstone, Jean Patterson, Jean Blacklock, unknown, Jean Hipgrave, unknown. Front row: Pat Charlton, Jean Gilbertson, unknown, Audrey Brown, unknown.

Spring Gardens School, 1948. Pictured, from left to right, back row: John Wear, unknown, Alan Readhead, Mr Turnbull (headmaster). Second row down: Miss Duxfield (teacher), unknown, Avril Gibson, Jean Hipgrave, Maureen Weatherstone, Audrey Brown, Jean Blacklock, Dorothy Pike. Second row up: Jean Patterson, Ann Wright, unknown, Jean Gilberston, Pat Charlton. Front row: unknown, Tom Ramshaw, Michael Oakey, unknown.

May Day celebrations at Spring Gardens School, c.1948–9. Pictured from left to right, back row: Unknown. Middle row: Sheena Barrett, Audrey Marshall, Jean Patterson, Avril Gibson. Front row: unknown, Jean Blacklock, Harry Davy, David Nichol.

Girls from King Edward's School, *c.*1932. The girls would have been born around 1920.

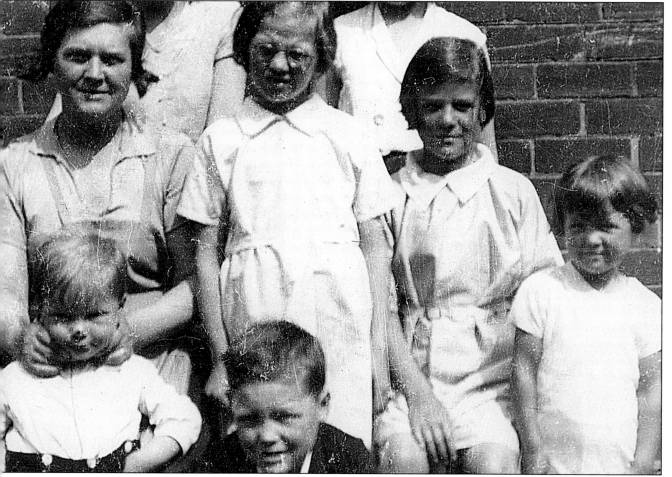

Mother and children from Landsdown Terrace, mid-1930s.

North Shields resident Harry Atkins found this photograph in a drawer, but he has no idea who the boy is in the picture, although he says the child is not one of his relatives. Harry's son Bernard was a keen photographer and it's highly probable that he snapped the boy while he was playing in the street. It was taken sometime around 1962. It is a fine example of two things. Firstly, what the old bikes looked like and secondly, the serenity of residential streets before the mass ownership of cars.

Maurice and Ellen Dawson, in Landsdown Terrace, North Shields, have fun on a bicycle in April 1935.

Two girls from North Shields have their photograph taken before heading off to a private school in Jesmond, 1947.

Children from the Western Board School relax in the summer sunshine. The Western Board School was demolished in 1978.

Two children play in the aftermarth of a rainstorm in North Shields in 1951. Pictured are brother and sister Sidney and Sheila Kerr.

King Edward School infants, pictured in 1910. Sombre faces all round except for a child in the front row with a grin.

The Hunter family pictured in a back alley in 1909. In 1986, all of these children were apparently still alive.

The varied faces of teachers at Linskill School, 1949. Jessie Patterson was the teacher at the time. She's in the bottom row, fourth from left.

The summer holiday break is not far off as pupils take their places for the annual King Edward Girls School photograph, 1948.

This excellent snap of children finding amusement on a horse and cart, on Tynemouth sands in the mid-1930s, was discovered as a negative, amongst bric-a-brac bought at a car-boot sale.

Teachers at King Edward Primary School during the late 1980s. The only gentleman is the odd one out!

King Edward School's standard 5 in 1909. Only surnames exist on the original photograph. Top row, from left to right: Mr G. Bavidge (teacher), Bulmer, unknown, Havery, unknown, G. Wayman, R. McNab. Middle row: G. Vyse, W. Jackson, Rogers, unknown, unknown, Front row: L. Eames, W.H. Boon, unknown, unknown, unknown.

Just look at those fashions. A King Edward Primary School photograph, *c.*1973. The children will be around 40 years old now.

Children from King Edward Junior School, pictured in 1987.

Ten-year-old boys from King Edward Primary School, in 1935.

King Edward Junior School children in 1987.

King Edward's School, 1911–12. The headmaster was G. Hurrell. Note the 'poor' boys without white collars.

Hats off! Children from King Edward School in 1984 celebrate the 75th anniversary of the school which was opened in 1909.

King Edward Primary School children in 1986. The teacher is Mrs Blackburn.

Incredible to believe but 80 years have passed since this school photograph was taken at King Edward Primary School, in 1922. It's possible that one or two may still be alive.

King Edward School children at the weekend High Borrans Outdoor Centre in the Lake District, an outdoor activity trip, in 1995. At High Borrans, pupils are involved in a wide range of activities, including, orienteering, hill walking, canoeing, and the Earthkeepers Environmental programme.

Girls from King Edward Primary School dress up in handmade grass skirts to enjoy an 'Hawian' day in 1986.

Children from King Edward Primary School swap their modern clothes to dress in the dour attire of the year 1910 for an Empire Day enactment in 1984.

Rule Brittania! In the same re-enactment this girl from King Edward Primary School finds out what Empire Day was really about.

The real thing. This is a King Edward School Empire Day celebration, *c.*1936. The interior of the school is relatively unchanged since then.

May Day celebrations at King Edward Primary School in 1984.

King Edward Primary School, 1989. Teachers are Mr Luccock and Mrs Smart.

King Edward Primary School in 1989. The ladies are Moira Furnace and Yvonne Hastie.

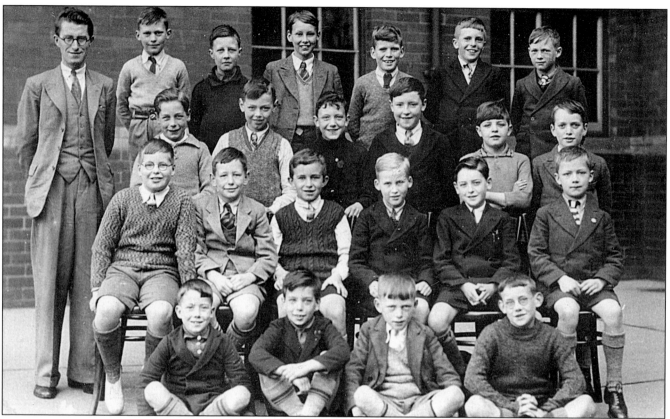

Children from King Edward Primary School, 1935. The old stiff white collars have given way to less formal clothes and strictness.

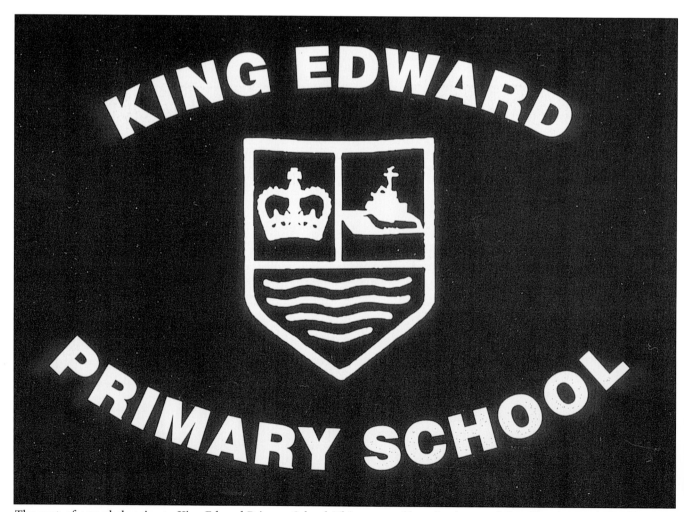

The coat-of-arms belonging to King Edward Primary School. This centre of learning is one of the oldest in North Shields.

In 1981 the wedding of the Prince of Wales and Lady Diana Spencer captured the nation's hearts and imagination. As a consequence, many schools throughout the UK celebrated the event in various ways, from parties to more inventive ways. King Edward Primary School hit on the excellent idea of staging their very own royal wedding. Here, two children act out the roles of Queen Elizabeth, Prince Phillip, Princes Charles and Princess Diana.

The King Edward Primary School 'royal' wedding of 1981. Here, the children act out the roles of bridesmaids.

Royal wedding, 1981. Two children act out the roles of Prince Charles and Princess Diana, formerly Lady Diana Spencer.

Another King Edward Primary School royal wedding picture, 1981. Two children act out the roles of Queen Elizabeth and Prince Phillip.

Thousands of schools across the country celebrated the royal wedding of 1981. It came not long after the Queen's silver jubilee of 1977.

King Edward Primary School in 1989. Children include Stephen Dodds, Mark Macciocchi and Naomi Thompson. The teacher is Mr McCallion.

Children from King Edward Primary School in 1989. The teacher is Mr Young.

Children don scary make-up for a 'Halloween Spooks' event at King Edward School during the early 1990s.

With a patriotic Union flag draped behind them, teachers from King Edward School proudly pose for their photograph in June 1909. The gentleman, third row up, second from the right, is the only one not looking directly at the camera.

All dressed up and ready to party. King Edward Primary School teachers' dance, *c.*1932.

Dinner ladies staff during the mid-1990s at King Edward Primary School.

King Edward's Boys' School (1925–6) annual staff photograph, taken December 1925. The white-haired headmaster appears to be a gentle figure.

Girls from the Western Board School, 1910. Pictured bottom row, second from right is Bertha Rutherford.

Long-time North Shields resident Ritchie Rutherford is pictured here with his mother Bertha, waiting at a bus stop in Tynemouth in 1952.

Under the watchful eyes of two adults, children from Spring Gardens Primary School try out a food can crusher which was won by parents at the Fish Quay Festival and presented by Deputy Mayor, Councillor Margaret Hall, in August 1994.

Queen Victoria School in Coach Lane, North Shields, 1948. Left to right, fifth along is Jimmy Bilton. Second row down, third from right, Alan O'Neil. Third row down: second from left, Judith Hetherington. Fifth along, Sheila Took. Bottom, third from left, Evelyn Baxter.

A class of all girls at Linskill School in 1951. Second row down, first on left, Maureen Kirkup, who now lives in Australia.

Collingwood School, Oswin Terrace, 1969. Jacqueline Hutchinson (née Lines), is second row up, third from right.

Sporting Themes

Tynemouth High School intermediate rugby team, 1951. Back row, from left to right: Gordon Limbrick, Ivan Matthews, unknown, George Rankin, unknown, Geoff Shepherd, unknown, Herbie Wakenshaw, Pud Sisterson, Alan Moore. Front row, from left to right: Mariner Purvis, unknown, Paul Smith, Colin Wilkinson, unknown, unknown, David Huitson.

East End Boys Club, North Shields, 1952–3. Back row, left to right: Arthur Stapely, Brian Morton, Eric Raffo. Middle row: Frank Raffo (Trainer), Colin Wilkinson, John Arnold, Sid Newton. Front row: Bill Southern, Bill Lamb, Les Shannon, Terry Boyle, Geordie Wright.

East End Boys Club, North Shields (1952–3), 1st and 2nd XI football teams. Back row, left to right: Joe Quinn, Harry Fernandes, Arthur Stapely, Brian Morton, George Willis, Peter Carr, Eric Raffo, Sid Hall. Top middle row: Mr Willis (trainer), Bill Wood, Tommy Young, Colin Wilkinson, John Arnold, Sid Newton, Billy Schofield, George Mullen. Second row: Bobby Southern, Billy Lamb, Bill Southern, Les Shannon, Terry Boyle, Geordie Wright, Bill Morton, Mr Frank Raffo (trainer). Front row: Barney Cuff, Charlie Spendiff, Jimmy Duck, Stand Whittaker, Arthur Bland.

Tynemouth High School rugby team, 1951. Back row: Unknown, Mick Oxnard, Ivan Matthews, George Rankin, Colin Wilkinson, Geoff Shephard, David Hall, unknown. Front row: Ron Cave, George Lisle, unknown, unknown, David Huitson, Mariner Purvis, Alan Moore.

Tynemouth High School football team, 1951–2. Back row, left to right: Arthur Stapely, Brian Chater, John Arnold, Eddie Leteve, Colin Wilkinson, Les Shannon. Front row: Alan Reed, Geoff Lisle, Mick Murray, Dick Maynes, John Armstrong, Alan Moore, Don Rutherford. Don eventually played full-back for the England rugby team.

Tynemouth High School senior rugby team, 1952. Back row, left to right: Mick Reed, Phil Bradbeer, unknown, unknown, unknown, unknown, Barry Mcquire, Colin Wilkinson, unknown. Front row: unknown, unknown, unknown, Carlton Johnson, unknown, Phil Tomaselli, David Huitson.

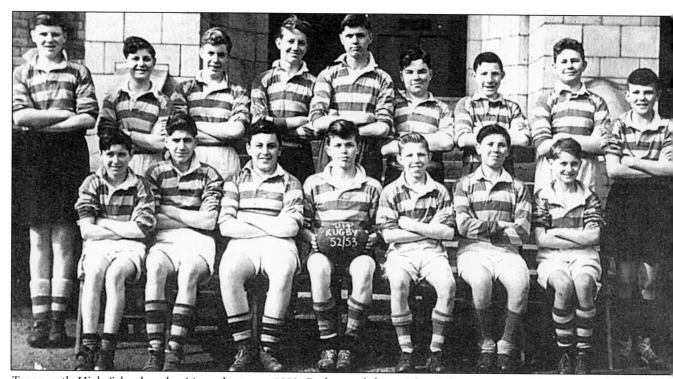

Tynemouth High School under-14s rugby team, 1953. Back row, left to right: Colin Snowdon, John Cooper, Frank Mavin unknown, unknown, Derek Hull, Edward Atkinson, unknown, John Potts. Front row: Albert Snowdon, Cyril Innes, unknown David Oxnard, Ralph Butler, George Renner.

The following twelve photographs are associated with Percy Park RFC. Pictured here is the popular P.F. Hardwick of England, Northumberland.

C.W. Russell was associated with Percy Park RFC. He was a record-breaking Northumberland holder of 56 county caps.

E.S. Scorfield, England, Northumberland.

W.D.G. Moran, England, Barbarians, Northumberland.

D. Rutherford, England, Barbarians, Northumberland, and Gloucestershire.

R. Macdonald, an all-rounder for Scotland, British Lions, Barbarians and Durham.

C.O. Robinson, England XV in South Africa, Barbarians.

H.C. Catchside, pictured in the early 1920s. He was Percy Park RFC's chairman and served on the English selection committee.

W. Wallace, British Lions, Northumberland, Percy Park *c*.1930.

G.C. Robinson, England, Barbarians, and Northumberland. He was president of the Rugby Union, 1939–40.

Newport RFC pay a visit to Percy Park in December 1952.

Swansea RFC on a visit to Preston Avenue in December 1955.

Members of the North Shields Athletic FC, season 1907–8. Players included E. Shotten, A. Robson, H. Thompson, F. Brown, H. Wardle and G. Hogg. The Alliance Cup is on the left.

North Shields Athletic FC, pictured in 1903. The gentleman in the back row with a bowler hat is Mr Taylor.

North Shields White Star Harriers, pictured in 1910. Their mascots were often the sons of the players.

A North Shields cricketer gets ready to bat in what is now known as the Preston Grange area.

Footballer of the Year in 1973 was 18-year-old Jim Weightman. A former pupil of Preston High School, North Shields, Jim managed to juggle both a successful amateur football career with working as a civil servant at Longbenton.

Flying high. Gymnast, Lorna Brown, then 18, of Fairfield Drive, Cullercoats, during a training session in 1966. Lorna was born in Tynemouth and left King Edward's School, North Shields, when she was 11 years old. A private tutor enabled her to concentrate on her chosen sport.

Anyone for tennis? A local lady dons her whites in what is now the Preston Grange area, *c*.1932.

King Edward School netball team, early 1990s.

Murton County Primary School netball team, 1959–60. Front row (far right) is Sheila Kerr.

King Edward School football team, mid-1990s. Among those pictured are Stephen Dodds, Andrew Dougal, Craig Lowdon, Jamie Moore, Richard Yates and Shaun Kirkbride.

King Edward School football team, 1994–5. Among those pictured are Thomas Nicholson, Lee Toby, Gareth Coulter, Craig Garner and Michael Pearson.

Girls from King
Edward Primary
School netball
team, 1985–6.

King Edward Primary School rugby team, cup winners in 1922–3.

King Edward's Boys' School rugby team, cup winners in 1924. The school has won countless cups over the years.

King Edward's Boys' School junior rugby players with their shield and cup, 1930–1.

King Edward's Boys' School rugby team, 1925–6. To this day, the school continues to enter football, netball, cricket, cross country, tag rugby, short tennis and athletic teams in local schools competitions and has enjoyed much success.

King Edward's Boys' School junior rugby team, 1947. Note the years were always written on the balls.

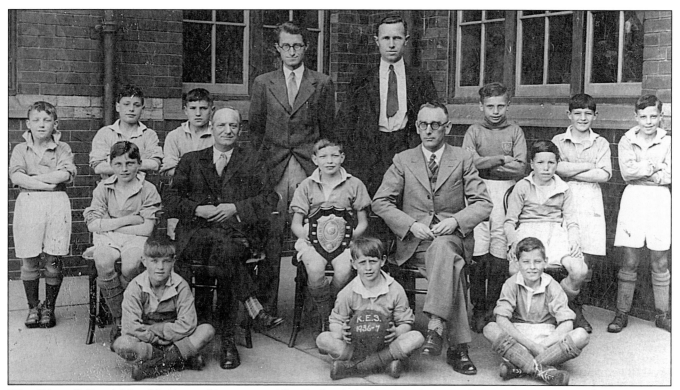

King Edward's Boys' School junior rugby team proudly display their winning plaque in the 1936–7 season.

King Edward's Boys' School juniors cricket champions, date unknown. The picture is faded but is framed and hangs in the school.

King Edward's Boys' School junior league champions, 1948–9. The boy third from the right on the front row, holds their winning shield.

King Edward's Boys' School junior rugby champions, 1958–9. These children will be around 60 years old by now – can you spot a face?

King Edward's Boys' School juniors, 1927–8. Children in their Brownie uniforms celebrate Empire Day.

King Edward's Boys' School junior rugby champions, 1927. Sadly, this photograph has faded badly over the years.

King Edward's Boys' School junior cricket team with their shield and cup. 1930–1.

Linskill School's successful netball team, pictured in 1962.